How to Write an Essay

Grades 7-12

Written by T. R. Gadd, B.A., M. Ed.
Illustrated by S&S Learnimg Materials

ISBN 1-55035-427-2
Copyright 1996
Revised January 2006
All Rights Reserved * Printed in Canada

Published in the United States by:
On the Mark Press
3909 Witmer Road PMB 175
Niagara Falls, New York
14305
www.onthemarkpress.com

Published in Canada by:
S&S Learning Materials
15 Dairy Avenue
Napanee, Ontario
K7R 1M4
www.sslearning.com

Look For Other Language Units

Table of Contents

This resource is designed to prepare and help students write essays in the first years of secondary school. It will be helpful for students at higher levels of education who have had difficulty with essay-writing in earlier years.

Because it teaches a basic formula approach to essay-writing, it is designed as a starting point only. If students expect to excel at essay-writing at the university level, they need to build on basics which are presented here. However, students who have never experienced success at writing essays will benefit from studying this resource.

Much of this resource is written from a students perspective, so that teachers may give students the pages which they need or so that students can purchase the book to use as they write their essays at home.

What is An Essay?

The word *essay* first came into use with the 1580 publication of a work entitled **Essais** by the French country-gentleman, Michel Eyquem de **MONTAIGNE**. It seems that Montaigne was a wealthy learned man who spent a great deal of his life reading the classics and writing about his philosophies of life. The word *essaai* comes from the French word *essayer*, meaning *to try*. An essay, therefore, is an **ATTEMPT** to persuade the reader to the writer's point of view.

The word **ESSAY** is also similar to the English word **ASSAY**. An *assay* is *a weighing of precious metal such as gold, in order to determine it purity. An essay, therefore, is a weighing of evidence in an attempt to convince the reader of the writer's point of view.*

Thus, an essay is essentially an argument, based on logic and evidence. The argument is developed through explanation, and the evidence, in the form of examples, quotations from expert sources, and illustrations, is explained in relationship to the argument.

After Montaigne, there were many other writers of essays. One of the most noteworthy of these writers was **SIR FRANCIS BACON**, whose essays showed a concise use of the English language in the early seventeenth century. An excerpt from an essay by Sir Francis Bacon appears on the following page. **PLEASE NOTE:** *Do no expect students to write the kinds of essays Bacon* wrote. These are the work of a genius, and although teachers should encourage students to aspire to greatness, there have been remarkably few writers in history who have shown an ability to emulate Bacon's works.

Of Love

By Sir Francis Bacon

The stage is more beholding to love than life of man. For as to the stage, love is ever a matter of comedies, and now and then tragedies, but in life it doth much mischief, sometimes like a siren, sometimes like a fury. You may observe that amongst all the great and worthy persons (whereof memory remaineth, either ancient or recent) there is not one that hath been transported to the mad degree of love: which shows that great spirits and great business do keep out this weak passion. You must accept nevertheless Marcus Antonius, the half partner of the empire of Rome, and Appius Claudius, the decemvir and lawgiver; whereof the former was indeed a voluptuous man and inordinate, but the ladder was an austere and wise man: and therefore it seems (although rarely) that into a heart well fortified, if watch be not kept. It is a poor saying of Epicurus, *Satis magnum alter alteri theatrum sumus* [One may find in ones neighbor a theater large enough], as if man, made for the contemplation of heaven and all noble objects, should do nothing but kneel before a little idol and make himself a subject, though not of the mouth (as beasts are), yet of the eye, which was given him for higher purposes. It is a strange thing to note the excess of this passion and how it braves the nature and value of things, by this: that the speaking in perpetual hyperbole is comely in nothing but in love. Neither is it merely in the phrase; for, whereas it hath been well said that an arch-flatterer, with whom all petty flatterers have intelligence, is a man's self, certainly the lover is more. For there was never proud man though so absurdly well of himself as the lover doth of the person loved; and therefore it was well said, "That it is impossible to love and to be wise." Neither doth this weakness appear to others only and not to the party loved, but to the loved most of all, except the love be reciprocal. For it is a true rule that love is ever rewarded either with the reciprocal or with an inward and secret contempt. By how much more men ought to beware of this passion which loseth not only other things but itself! As for the other losses, the poet's relation doth well figure them: that he that preferred Helena quitted and gifts of Juno and Pallas. For whosoever esteemeth too much of amorous affection quitteth both riches and wisdom. This passion hath his floods in the very times of weakness, which are greatly prosperity and great adversity, though this ladder hath been less observed: both which time kindle love and make it more fervent, and therefore show it to be the child of folly. They do best who, if they cannot but admit love, yet make it keep quarter, and sever it wholly from their serious affairs and actions of life; for it if checked once with business, it troubleth men's fortune and maketh men that they can no ways be true to their own ends. I know not how, but martial men are given to love. I think it is but as they are given to wine; for perils commonly ask to be paid in pleasures. There is in mans nature a secret inclination and motion towards love of others, which, if it be not spent upon some one or a few, doth naturally spread itself towards many, and maketh men become human and charitable, as it is seen sometime in friars. Nuptial love maketh mankind, friendly love perfecteth it, but wonton love corrupteth and embaseth it.

The Essay and the Report

An **ESSAY** as used in this resource means a **PERSUASIVE ESSAY** or **ARGUMENT**. Often students in school are asked to write a **REPORT**, this is, a summary of research findings without a specifically expressed argument.

Arguments and Reports differ in **PURPOSE** and in **ORGANIZATION**.

	ESSAY	REPORT
PURPOSE	• to be subjective: to argue a specific point of view • to provide evidence to support this point of view	• to be objective: to present findings from research • to provide examples from the research
ORGANIZATION	• statement of thesis: overall argument and supporting arguments • explanation of each argument in turn, followed by presentation of evidence and examples • conclusion	• statement of scope and purpose of the report • summary of findings citing examples and sources • conclusion and recommendations if required

Thus, a **REPORT** tends to be explanatory, whereas an **ESSAY** is persuasive or argumentative. A report may require a point of view or argument to be presented only if recommendations are required; and essay always requires a point of view or argument.

Examples of Essays and Reports

Various topics in secondary school courses lend themselves to essays; others lend themselves to reports. Students should ask their teachers if an argument or a report is required if there is any doubt as to the purpose of a given assignment. Many teachers use the word "essay" in a general sense to indicate a piece of writing, either persuasive or explanatory. Students, therefore, need to ensure that they are doing the kind of writing which the teacher requires.

What follows on the next page are some topics which students may encounter in various secondary school courses. The chart shows the different approaches to be taken if a persuasive essay or a report is required.

Students should note once again that essays take a particular point of view and argue it, whereas reports generally only provide explanation.

Samples of Essays and Report Topics

	ESSAY	REPORT
Topic 1: The Senate	• The Senate should be abolished. • The Senate performs a useful check on government.	• The organization of the Senate, including number of members, how they are appointed, what areas they represent, etc.
Topic 2: Erosion	• A particular planting technique is more helpful than another in preventing soil erosion. • Many economic disasters might have been averted if farmers had taken measures to control erosion.	• The advantages and disadvantages of various methods to control erosion. • Areas of the earth where erosion poses particular problems to the way of life of the inhabitants.
Topic 3: Women in Literature	• Women in literature are depicted as weak individuals defeated by their environment. • Shakespeare's women are extremes, either pretty ornaments or domineering tyrants.	• Examples of women who have written important pieces of literature and summaries of their lives. • Biographies of female characters in the works of a particular writer.

Activity #1: Essay and Report Topics

A) Some of the following topics would make good essays; others are more suitable for reports. In groups of two or three students, decide which are essay topics and which are report topics. Provide reasons for each decision and come to consensus as a group.

1. In William Shakespeare's play, <u>Romeo and Juliet</u>, the central characters are victims of fate.

2. There were many causes of world war one.

3. Macbeth is more a victim of his own character than a man controlled by outside forces.

4. Reasons why we should or should not recycle garbage.

5. The government, economy and society of Guyana.

6. The original ending of <u>Great Expectations</u> is superior to the revised ending.

7. A university graduate can expect a wider range of career options than a person with a high school diploma.

8. All rocks on earth can be classified as igneous, sedimentary, or metamorphic.

B) Following are some general subjects which could be used for either essays or reports. For each subject, phrase a specific essay topic and a specific report topic.

1. The United Nations
2. The major character in a novel or play which you have studied.
3. The economy of any country in the world.
4. Teenage pregnancy
5. The breakdown of the family in North America
6. Career opportunities
7. The lyrics of today's rock songs
8. Television

The Parts of an Essay

The argument of an essay is expressed in what writers call the THESIS. A thesis is the expression of the overall argument and the developing arguments of an essay. A thesis consists of two parts: proposition and issues.

The overall argument of the essay is called the PROPOSITION. The proposition is a general statement of argument; it does not provide details. In addition, a proposition is an opinion, not a fact, since a fact is not arguable.

The details are provided by the supporting argument, called ISSUES. The issues are the reason why he proposition may be considered valid. If the writer is able to prove that issues are valid and it the issues cover all the major arguments, then the proposition may be considered valid.

```
┌─────────────────────┐
│ PROPOSITION         │
└─────────────────────┘
```
is true because
```
┌─────────────────────┐
│ ISSUE 1             │
├─────────────────────┤
│ ISSUE 2             │
├─────────────────────┤
│ ISSUE 3, etc.       │
└─────────────────────┘
```
are true.

The thesis is based on evidence. EVIDENCE consists of examples, quotations, appeals to authority of any kind, statistics, logic—anything which will prove the validity of an issue.

On the following pages are examples of a thesis, divided into proposition and issues.

Thesis Examples

1. PROPOSITION:

Women are superior to men.

ISSUES:

1. Women are physically stronger than men.

2. Women are emotionally more stable than men.

3. Women are more intelligent than men.

4. Women are socially more adaptable than men.

Note that these issues and the proposition are opinions, not facts. This means that they can be argued. The same case could be made in reverse. The issues appear to cover all the major arguments which define superiority. If the writer of this particular essay is able to find evidence to support each of the issues, then the proposition can be assumed to be valid.

2. PROPOSITION:

In William Shakespeare's play, <u>Julius Caesar</u>, Brutus is more a character to be admired than one to be scorned.

ISSUES:

1. Brutus possesses qualities which have already earned him a good reputation in Rome.

2. In addition, Brutus is concerned with the good of others rather than possessing selfish motives.

3. Brutus acts according to his qualities and values.

A person taking this stand would argue that Brutus is a victim of others who use his good qualities for their own political ends; these are the ones who scorn him. The audience, on the other hand, sees Brutus's admirable qualities, even if these qualities may lead to his downfall.

Evidence

Evidence in an essay may take several forms:

1. Examples:

These are the most common types of evidence used in student essay writing. Any claim in an essay should be substantiated, and an example provides perhaps the best and easiest substantiation. In order to support the claim that Julius Caesar is arrogant, one might cite the example that he refuses to listen to the advice of the Soothsayer on the way to the Roman Senate on the Ides of March.

2. Quotations:

Quotations support the examples and should be used whenever possible in this support position. One might argue that Marc Antony is an example of the men who admire Brutus by quoting Antony's line, "This was the noblest Roman of them all."

3. Appeals to Authority:

An authority is a recognized expert on the topic of the essay, and his or her opinion can help to substantiate an argument. Students should note that not all authorities agree; essays after all do deal with opinion. On the other hand, the opinion of one who has spent a great deal of time studying the subject cannot be dismissed out of hand. Each field of learning has its own authorities, and students may research these and quote from them. Of course, any quotations or paraphrasing of an expert's views must be documented. Since there are a number of acceptable forms of documentation, students should always check with the teacher to see which formats are expected or acceptable.

4. Statistics And Illustrations:

Statistics and illustrations are forms of examples. If a student uses statistics in an essay, he or she should be sure to document the source of those statistics. Avoid making up statistics, such as "everyone knows..." or " statistics show...", unless these are documented. Illustrations are stories used to illustrate a point, and they may be taken from student's own experiences. However, students should avoid using the word "I" in a formal essay; in a personal essay, the word "I" is quite acceptable.

EVIDENCE (Continued)

5. Logic:

Arguments are often developed by logic. Logic essentially means that if argument A is true, then argument B follows. Logic is based on two types of reasoning: inductive and deductive.

A person who uses **inductive reasoning** observes as much of the world as possible, and then forms a conclusion based on these observations. If, for example, one were to observe swans in their native habitat in North America, South America, Europe, Africa, and Asia, one might form the conclusion that all swans are white. This theory would appear to be true based on thousands of observations in the places mentioned. However, if one observed swans in Australia, one would encounter black swans. Thus, inductive reasoning -- forming a conclusion based on observations -- may lead to a conclusion which is true or not true. Writers should, therefore, beware of making generalizations based on little observations.

Deductive reasoning begins with a general statement which is then applied to a specific situation in order to form a conclusion. If, for expel, one forms a conclusion based on inductive reasoning that all sheep are purple (not that this is a faulty premise), then this statement may be applied to a specific animal: this animal is a sheep. Thus, one can draw the conclusion that this animal is purple.

Note the following logical fallacy based on deductive reasoning:

All sheep are purple. [This statement is false.]

This animal is a sheep. [This animal is actually a peacock; therefore, the statement is false.]

This animal is purple. [In spite of two false statements, the conclusion is true.]

Students need to take care to avoid both faulty premises and generalizations which cannot be substantiated.

Note also that Sherlock Holmes often said to Dr. Watson, "brilliant deduction." In most cases, he should have said, "brilliant <u>in</u>duction."

PREWRITING

It is very difficulty to sit down and write an effective essay without doing any preplanning. Many educators consider the first stage of the writing process to be the most important.

Prewriting for an essay consists of four parts:

1. Brainstorming
2. Research
3. Selection of argument
4. Prewriting Plan

1. BRAINSTORMING:

The first stage of the writing process, after choosing the topic, is the brainstorming stage. At this point, a student has a topic but no arguments, although certain arguments may come to mind. The purpose of this stage is to use what the student already knows to begin to compile information which will be used for both arguments and evidence.

At the brainstorming stage, the student writes down on a piece of paper any information which pertains to the topic as these ideas come into his or her mind. The student may use mind-mapping techniques if these are easier. It is often a good idea to set a quantity goal -- for example, four pages of brainstorming for an essay up to 1 000 words -- so that the student does not stop short.

What follows is an example of brainstorming for an essay on the topic "Is Brutus in Julius Caesar, a character to be admired or scorned?"

admired -- liked [check dictionary for definition], worthy of praise, regarded with
       wonder or delight.

scorned -- disliked, looked down on, despised

kills Caesar

for the good of Rome?

the noblest Roman [check quotation]

had to be killed -- stupid plan

made many mistakes, etc.

PREWRITING (Continued)

2. RESEARCH:

Research involves using both primary and secondary sources.

The **Primary Source** in a literary essay is the work of literature on which the essay is based; for example, <u>Julius Caesar</u> is the work of literature for the topic listed on the last page. Some teachers of English require essays based only on a primary source; there may be no primary sources for essays in other subject areas.

The **Secondary Sources** are works written **about** the primary source or the topic of the essay. There are many books available about works of literature; for example, Prentice-Hall has published a series of books on various writers and various works, called <u>Twentieth Century Views</u> and <u>Twentieth Century Interpretations</u>. The school library often has several of these types of works available. In other subjects, such as History, Geography or Science, there are many books about the subject. These range from encyclopedias and other general reference books to books dealing with the specific topic. Students should be encouraged to check the card catalog or computer system to see what is available. Finally, the computer itself provides many secondary sources, through various programs and the Internet. Students should always check with the teachers to see if secondary sources are required or acceptable.

In the **Research** stage of the writing process, students should write down any quotations or paraphrases which have a bearing on the topic. They should also include examples which they can later paraphrase in the essay. They need to be sure to note the work and page number of each source. Here are some examples for the essay on Brutus, started in the brainstorming section on the previous page:

"This was the noblest Roman of them all." (Act V, scene v, Line 68)

Act III, scene ii, Lines 75-101: Antony repeatedly refers to Brutus as "an honorable man".

Act IV, Scene iii, Lines 217-218: "There is a tide in the affairs of men/Which, taken at the flood, leads on to fortune."

Act II, Scene i: Brutus refuses to tell his wife, Portia, about the assassination plot in order to protect her.

PREWRITING (Continued)

3. SELECTION OF ARGUMENTS:

After completing several pages of brainstorming and research, the student should begin to see specific arguments emerging. Now is the time to make preliminary statements of arguments.

The student will begin by stating the **Proposition** -- the over all argument of the essay. Usually, the essay topic is phrased so that it presents two opposing propositions. Some such topics are:

- Is Brutus a man to be admired or a fool?
- Should the Senate be abolished?

Topics such as these generally require yes or no answers. Other topics are more general and require students to create a proposition from the topic. A question such as, "What was the primary cause of World War I" requires the student to make a judgment, to offer an opinion. Research and brainstorming might focus on one cause more then others, thus allowing the student to form judgment more easily. Topics which are incomplete sentences require more thought from the writer; for example, a topic such as "The growth of nationalism in the United States before the American Revolution" will ask students to create their own arguments based on the research they have found; with such a topic, the brainstorming should include helpful questions such as:

- "What events created nationalistic feelings?"
- "Which events were the most significant?"
- "What leaders contributed to the nationalistic movement?"

Questions like these will make it easier for the student to phrase a proposition.

The next step is to phrase potential **Issues**. Issues are supporting arguments which state **why** the Proposition is valid. They are the **reason**. At this stage, the issues are only **potential** arguments which may or may not be used in the essay.

Once the potential issues are stated, the student may combine some of these into one final issue. An essay will contain two or more issues; three is a good number, but students must remember that each issue will form a paragraph. Not all essays will be five paragraphs in length; the number of paragraphs will be determined by the number of issues.

PREWRITING (Continued)

4. PREWRITING PLAN:

The **Prewriting Plan** may be the most important step in writing an essay, for it is at this stage that the writer can clarify arguments, their development and their support. If it is done well, the prewriting plan shows the entire essay on one sheet of paper. Students should use larger sheets of paper for longer essays.

The typical prewriting plan looks as follows:

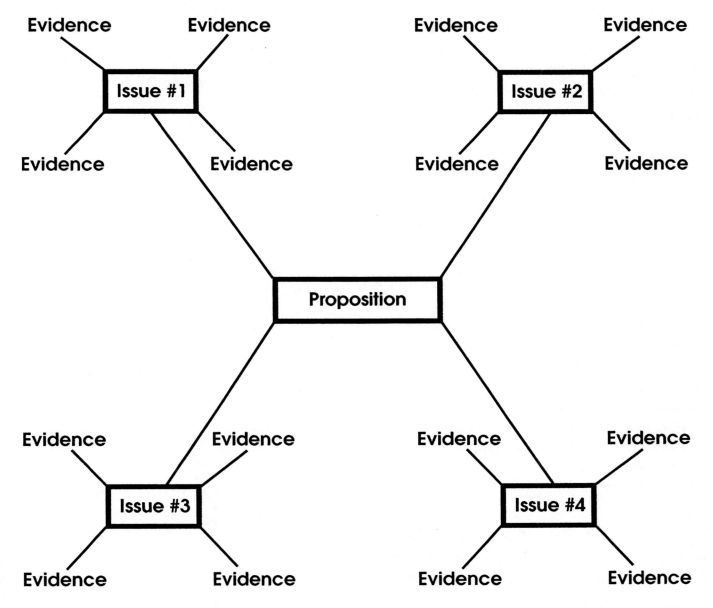

4. PREWRITING PLAN (Continued):

A partial plan for the essay on Brutus follows:

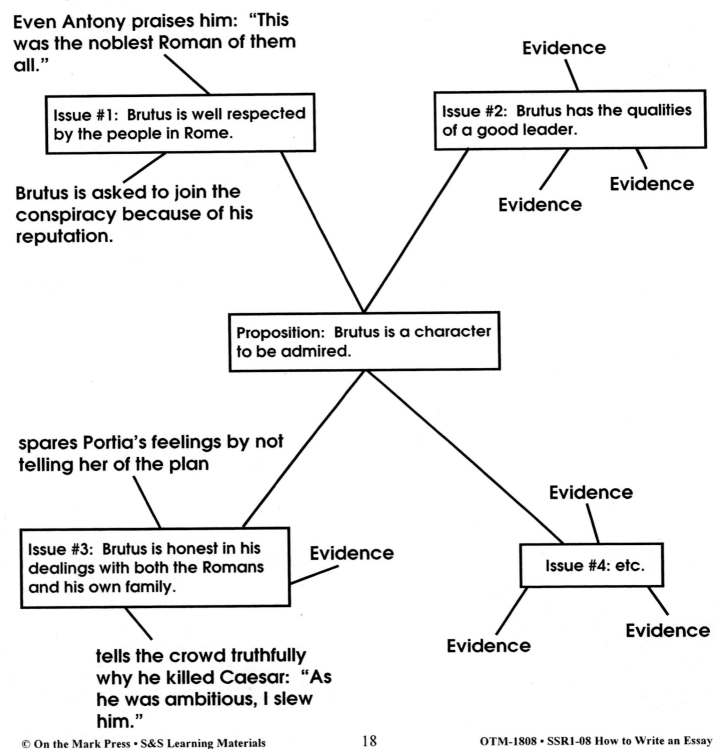

Even Antony praises him: "This was the noblest Roman of them all."

Evidence

Issue #1: Brutus is well respected by the people in Rome.

Issue #2: Brutus has the qualities of a good leader.

Brutus is asked to join the conspiracy because of his reputation.

Evidence

Evidence

Proposition: Brutus is a character to be admired.

spares Portia's feelings by not telling her of the plan

Evidence

Issue #3: Brutus is honest in his dealings with both the Romans and his own family.

Evidence

Issue #4: etc.

Evidence

tells the crowd truthfully why he killed Caesar: "As he was ambitious, I slew him."

Evidence

Writing the First Draft

Most students who have difficulty writing essays need to work on content and organization; style will come later; and mechanics can be helped by proofreading, editing or using one of the many computer programs. The steps in the Prewriting stage will help to provide adequate content for the essay. What follows is a simple pattern which should help the student organize the essay. When the student is thoroughly familiar with the pattern, this formula can then be changed to meet the individual student's needs.

1. THE THESIS PARAGRAPH:

• **Step 1:** Begin with a sentence which catches the reader's interest. This sentence should not be the proposition for the essay, but should be somewhat related to the topic. The idea of the opening sentence may be developed or explained in several sentences which follow it.

• **Step 2:** In a literary essay it is necessary to state the title and author of the work on which the essay is based (e.g. William Shakespeare's Julius Caesar). This statement may be included in the same sentence which states the proposition (see step 3). Of course, in a non-literary essay this step would be omitted.

• **Step 3:** State the proposition in a single sentence. Do not explain the proposition at this point unless it is absolutely necessary to do so. The proposition can be explained as the issues are developed later in the essay.

• **Step 4:** State each issue in a separate sentence for each. If the issues are simple, they may be combined into a single sentence. However, a separate sentence for each one emphasizes the importance of each issue.

• **Step 5:** Conclude the paragraph by restating the proposition.

Following this pattern ensures that the arguments are clear to the reader or evaluator of the essay. By the end of the first paragraph, the reader knows what will be argued (the proposition) and how this argument will be developed (the issues).

A sample thesis paragraph appears on page 21.

WRITING THE FIRST DRAFT (Continued)

2. TRANSITIONS:

Simply following the pattern on page 19 will result in a thesis paragraph which is choppy without any coherent flow. **Coherence** is a logical flow of ideas and relies on connective words and phrases to create this flow. These connective words and phrases are called **transitions**.

Transitions are used in the thesis paragraph mainly to connect issues. Beginning with the second issue, transitional words and phrases create coherence. They are also used to connect paragraphs in the body of the essay, beginning with the second issue, much as they are used in the thesis paragraph.

The most obvious transition words list issues in the order in which they will appear in the essay. These are "number" words, such as:

- first
- secondly
- thirdly, etc..

As stated, these transitions are obvious and would be avoided by more experienced writers.

Better transitions are words and phrases such as the following:

• in addition	} These transitions are used
• similarly	} to connect issues which are
• also	} similar arguments.
• likewise	}
• on the other hand	> These transitions are used
• on the contrary	> to connect opposite ideas.
• however	>
• therefore	} These transitions are useful
• thus, etc.	} before a concluding sentence.

Transitions which begin paragraphs will sometimes **repeat** the idea of the preceding paragraph as the writer leads into the next major idea.

WRITING THE FIRST DRAFT (Continued)

3. A SAMPLE THESIS PARAGRAPH:

What follows is a thesis paragraph based on the proposition that "Women are superior to men." Note that it follows all the steps in the pattern on page 19.

Statement to catch the reader's interest

Statement of propsition

Statement of each issue, beginning with transitions

From the time when Eve first handed Adam the apple, women have had the controlling hand in the male-female relationship. In fact, women are superior to men. First of all, women are more intelligent than men. Similarly, women are physically stronger than men. In addition, women are emotionally more stable than men. Finally, women are more socially adaptable than

Summation restating the proposition

men. Thus, it is clear that women are superior to men.

This is a very simple thesis paragraph, designed to show the pattern. Note that it is very repetitive, particularly in the repetition of the words "women" and "men". It might be advisable for the writer to find synonyms for these words. On the other hand, the thesis is stated very strongly through all of this repetition; the writer's thesis is absolutely clear to the reader.

WRITING THE FIRST DRAFT (Continued)

4. PARAGRAPHS IN THE BODY OF THE ESSAY:

Paragraphs in the body of the essay follow a pattern to maintain unity and coherence. Unity means that there is one idea per paragraph; normally, this is the issue which the paragraph is developing. If the issue is particularly long (in an essay of more than 5 000 words, for example), the issue will be stated in an introductory paragraph which also subdivides the issues into several component parts; each component part will then comprise one paragraph; a concluding paragraph will summarize the issue and its component parts before the writer moves on to the next issue. In a shorter essay (the kind that most secondary school students are expected to write), this will not be a problem; each issue will comprise one paragraph. **Coherence** will be achieved through the use of transitions—words, phrases or sentences, as required by the essay.

A typical paragraph for the essay will follow these steps:

- **Step 1:** Starting with a transition, state the issue in a single sentence.

- **Step 2:** Explain the issue as necessary. The issue may be self explanatory and may need no further explanation. On the other hand, the issue may require one or several sentences for explanation.

- **Step 3:** Provide evidence to support the issue. This evidence may be a quotation or an example.

- **Step 4:** Explain how the evidence supports the issue. This explanation may require one or several sentences.

- **Step 5:** Repeat steps 3 and 4 for each piece of evidence.

- **Step 6:** Sum up the issue and refer to the proposition.

This pattern will be followed for each paragraph in the essay. Students need to remember that each paragraph develops one of the issues in the essay. Thus, an essay with three issues will be five paragraphs in length ·· an introductory paragraph, one paragraph for each of the three issues and a concluding paragraph. An essay with four issues will be six paragraphs in length, and so on.

WRITING THE FIRST DRAFT (Continued)

5. THE CONCLUDING PARAGRAPH:

A concluding paragraph should sum up the arguments of the essay and emphasize the proposition. The simplest method of writing a concluding paragraph is as follows:

- **Step 1:** Beginning with a transition, restate the proposition.

- **Step 2:** Restate each issue in turn in the order in which they were developed in the essay. It is not necessary to use a separate sentence for each issue in the concluding paragraph.

- **Step 3:** Restate the proposition.

The concluding paragraph may contain a sentence (or several sentences) which state why the proposition is important. This may mean that the writer will apply the argument to his own world in order to show its relevance.

A concluding paragraph will never contain new information (other than the application described in the previous paragraph), as any new information should have been included in the essay in the first place.

6. THE PATTERN:

The pattern shown here may produce essays which are very repetitive. Students should try to avoid a great deal of repetition by finding other ways of saying the same thing. They should not feel restricted by the pattern, but should learn to adapt the pattern to their own style.

On the other hand, following this pattern will produce an essay which is well organized; that is, it is unified, coherent and emphatic. Once students have learned this structure, teachers should ensure that they develop the pattern to incorporate their individual needs and creativity. Like any artist learning perspective, students should learn the pattern; when they have mastered it, they are ready to become artists.

WRITING THE FIRST DRAFT (Continued)

7. USING QUOTATIONS IN THE ESSAY:

It would be unusual for an essay to have no quotations, because quotations are references to specific sources. As such, they provide evidence which is forceful and direct.

Short quotations (less than three lines in length) are incorporated into the normal sentence structure. An example follows:

> Brutus is even acknowledged by his arch-enemy, Marc Antony, as a man
>
> worthy of respect. Antony says of Brutus, "This was the noblest Roman
>
> of them all", even after he has witnessed the death of Brutus.

Note that the essay is double-spaced. It is normal to double-space any essay which is to be submitted for evaluation. It is advisable that students double-space even the first draft of the essay, so that they can make hand-written revisions as necessary. If the essay is written on a word-processor (the recommended method, since it makes revisions an easy task), the first draft should be double-spaced.

Long quotations (three lines or more) are indented and single-spaced; quotation marks are omitted. An example follows:

> Brutus is even acknowledged by his arch-enemy, Marc Antony,
>
> as a man worthy of respect. Antony says of Brutus:
>
>> This was the noblest Roman of them all….
>> His life was gentle, and the elements
>> So mix'd in him, that Nature might stand up
>> And say to all the world, "This was a man!"
>
> If the enemy of Brutus, who worked so hard to capture or kill him,
>
> can speak so admirably of him, then it is clear that Brutus is a man
>
> to be respected.

WRITING THE FIRST DRAFT (Continued)

7. USING QUOTATIONS IN THE ESSAY (Continued):

The quotations cited on the last page are poetry, and therefore the line lengths of the original are preserved. In a short quotation, a slash (/) is used to separate two lines:

> Brutus is even acknowledged by his arch-enemy, Marc Antony,
>
> as a man worthy of respect. Antony says of Brutus, "All the
>
> conspirators save only he/Did that they did in envy of great
>
> Caesar" even after he has witnessed the death of Brutus.

Dots are used in quotations to indicate words that have been omitted. This is a particularly useful device if the quotation is very long and says more than the writer of the essay wants to use. Three dots (...) indicate that a word or several words have been omitted. However, if a period occurs in the omitted words, four dots (....) are used to indicate that part of a sentence or more has been omitted. Students should realize that it is clearly dishonest to use dots to change the sense of the quotation being cited. One cannot, for example, take a quotation such as, "Brutus is not an honorable man", and quote it as, "Brutus is...an honorable man."

Sometimes words need to be inserted into a quotation, particularly if it is necessary to incorporate the pronoun into the sentence of the essay or to indicate a person referred to in the quotation. Inserted words are placed in brackets [ ]. Note: Brackets are always square, whereas parentheses are round. An example follows: "This [Brutus] was the noblest Roman of them all." Again brackets should be used honestly.

WRITING THE FIRST DRAFT (Continued)

8. FOOTNOTES AND BIBLIOGRAPHY:

Although it is important to cite sources of information, the format for doing so (using footnotes and bibliography) seems to be highly contentious. There are teachers and university professors who insist on a particular format; they believe that any format but the one they want is wrong. Sometimes this attitude results in lower grades for students essays. It is absolutely essential, therefore, for students to ask their teachers or professors what format is required.

There are many books written on format for footnotes and bibliography and these are available in most secondary school, college and university libraries.

Footnotes traditionally are placed at the foot of a page. They may be placed on a separate page at the end of an essay, as this is often a simpler procedure to use with a typewriter or word processor. If they are placed on a separate page, the page should be headed, "Endnotes" rather than "Footnotes".

A simple format for footnotes follows:

Raised number (beginning with 1 and continuing consecutively), author of work, title (underlined), page number (with page or p. inserted or omitted). Note the punctuation required.

[1]Charles Dickens, <u>Great Expectations</u>, p. 54.

Some teachers or professors prefer that students do not use footnotes, but rather use the author's surname and the page number placed in parentheses, for example: (Dickens, 54). Still others like the date of publication included, as in (Dickens, 1861, p. 54). Some like the "p"; others don't. Confused? You should be; there are so many methods, and for some inexplicable reason the format chosen may be a major bone of contention for a particular university professor. Again, it is important for students to ask their teachers or professor which format is required.

WRITING THE FIRST DRAFT (Continued)

8. FOOTNOTES AND BIBLIOGRAPHY (Continued):

For some reason, Bibliography is not as contentious an issue as footnotes. Most teachers and professors agree on the following format:

Author's surname, Author's first name. <u>Title of Work</u> (underlined). City of Publications; Publisher, year of publication. An example follows:

Dickens, Charles. <u>Great Expectations</u>. New York; The MacMillan Company Limited, 1965.

Most of this information is found on the first two pages of a book, the front piece or title page and the page which follows it. When an international publisher is involved, there may be several cities of publication. The student should cite the city in the country in which he resides or the city closest to him. The student should also cite the year of the last edition of the book, not the year of the last printing of the book.

Works cited in the Bibliography should be listed in alphabetical order according to the first word of the reference. Some references, for example, have no author. A reference for <u>The Holy Bible</u> would begin with the title of the work rather than the author's surname.

Title's of full length works -- such as books, movies, magazines, or encyclopedia entries -- are underlined. Titles of articles within these works (e.g. short stories, magazine or newspaper articles, encyclopedia entries) are placed in quotation marks. Signed articles in such works begin with the author's name; undersigned articles omit the author's name. An example follows:

Gadd, David. "The World of Baseball". <u>Sports For All</u>. Oshawa; S&S Publishers, 1996

If the article were unsigned, the author's name would simply be omitted.

EDITING AND REVISING

Editing and revising are not merely proof-reading. Rather they comprise a very important step in the writing process at which stage the student will do a thorough evaluation of his or her writing and will receive feedback from teachers, peers or parents. Students need to be taught **how** to edit; they should not simply be expected to know how to do it. Unless students are taught how to edit, peer edits will consist of comments like "Good work" or "Check spelling"—and these comments are of little practical use in improving a piece of writing.

Students often have more difficulty editing their own work that editing someone else's work. It is, therefore, good practice for students to peer edit, not only to help the other student to improve, but also to learn how to improve their own writing.

A **sample editing sheet** for an essay appears on page 30. This sheet may be used for both self- and peer-editing. Students should write the comments for each category, question or statement on a sheet of paper separate from the essay. A peer-edit for an essay may run from four to six pages in length, if the editor writes comments for everything on the editing sheet. Encourage students to write edits of sufficient length to be helpful to the writer of the essay and to test their own skills.

The editing sheet examines the essay under four categories -- Organization, Content, Style and **Mechanics**. This unit has already looked at Organization and Content in some detail. Style and Mechanics are covered in the following pages.

The Organization section of the editing sheet reviews the pattern taught in this unit. The peer editor (or writer) should first ask if the essay follows the pattern. If it does, then the writer need only write under the heading "Organization"; "Follows the pattern taught in class." If it does not follow the pattern, the editor needs to ask; "Does the writer's pattern work?" If the answer is "Yes", then the editor should be prepared to explain in what ways the essay is effective without following the pattern. If the answer is "No", then the editor will point out where the essay fails to follow the pattern.

EDITING AND REVISING (Continued)

1. A SAMPLE EDITING SHEET FOR AN ESSAY:

Organization:

THESIS PARAGRAPH:
1. begins with a statement which catches the reader's interest
2. states title and author work
3. states proposition clearly in a single sentence
4. states each issue clearly in a separate sentence for each
5. sums up proposition
6. uses transitions throughout

BODY PARAGRAPH:
1. uses transitions to tie each paragraph to the preceding paragraph
2. states issue at beginning of each paragraph
3. explains the issue as necessary
4. provides evidence
5. clearly shows how evidence supports its respective issue
6. sums up issue
7. refers to proposition

CONCLUSION:
1. restates each issue
2. restates proposition
3. adds no new information

CONTENT:
1. Are all the important arguments covered and explained?
2. Does the evidence clearly prove the issues?
3. Is any important evidence or argument omitted?
4. Is the controlling idea of the proposition carried through each issue and evidence?

STYLE:
1. Are the sentences varied in length and structure?
2. Are the words chosen precise and effective?
3. Are nouns and verbs precise and effective?
4. Is the language level appropriate to the intended audience of the essay?
5. Is the tone appropriate?
6. Are focus and emphasis correct in important sentences?
7. Is subordination effective in emphasizing the main idea?
8. Is parallel structure used effectively?
9. Is the syntax varied?

MECHANICS:
1. Are there any errors in spelling, grammar or sentence structure?
2. Are footnotes, bibliography and quotations used according to accepted format?
3. Are there adequate margins on right, left, top and bottom?
4. Is the essay double-spaced and written or typed on one side of each page?
5. Is there a title page?

2. STYLE:

We often use the word style in reference to fashion, as in *style of clothes*. A person with style is said to possess a knowledge of the latest trends, a certain flair. In writing, style refers to the way the writer uses **language** to create specific effects or to reach certain goals.

> Thus, style is the use of words and the arrangement of words to form sentences.

a) Sentence Variation:

Sentences can vary in both length and structure.

Sentences can be long or short. A series of short sentences or a series of long sentences will produce one of several particular effects:

- Short sentences can convey an impression of speed or haste. Look at the *following series of sentences: I peered through the window. He was there.* He saw me. I started to run. He came after me. The repetition of short sentences conveys speed to the reader; there is no time to consider because the action is fast.

- *Short sentences can also convey a simple, childlike attitude. I saw the strawberry. It looked good. I reached for it. I put it into my mouth. It* tasted nice. These sentences give the impression that the writer or speaker is a very young child. If this is the effect the writer wishes to convey, then the repetition of short sentences is effective; if the writer does not wish to convey this impression, then the choice of short sentences is poor style. effective; if the writer does not wish to convey this impression, then the choice of short sentences is poor style.

- Long sentences are more thoughtful, sometimes even ponderous and slow. *As I peered through the window and saw him there, I knew that he saw me also, and at that moment I started to run, with him in hot pursuit of me.* Notice that the effect of speed is lost, although there is a certain sense of intellectualism in the description.

- Sometimes long sentences can be used to create suspense if the subject *and verb are not stated until the end of the sentence. Over the hills and into the valleys, across the streams and rivers, into the towns and villages* stormed the soldiers. Notice that the subject follows even the verb at the **end** of this sentence; the reader is left in suspense. This kind of sentence is called a **Periodic** sentence.

EDITING AND REVISING (Continued)

2. STYLE (Continued):

a) Sentence Variation (Continued):

- Loose sentences, on the other hand are more natural that Periodic sentences. In a loose sentence, the subject and verb appear earlier in the sentence. *The soldiers stormed over the hills and into the valleys, across the streams and rivers, into the towns and villages.* A loose sentence like this one is simple and clean; the reader grasps the message immediately.

- In an essay it is often a good idea to **vary** the sentence lengths and arrangements. An essay composed of all short sentences, or all long sentences, or all periodic sentences, or all loose sentences is not likely to be as effective as one which uses sentence variety.

Sentences should also vary in structure. Structure refers to the selection and number of principal and subordinate clauses in a sentence.

- A **simple** sentence contains only one principal clause and no subordinate clause. *Like peaches and pears* is a simple sentence.

- A **compound** sentence contains two or more principal clauses, but no subordinate clauses. *I like peaches and pears, but I am allergic to fruit* is a compound sentence. The writer is saying that both these ideas are of equal importance.

- A **complex** sentence contains one principal clause and one or more subordinate clauses. *Although I like peaches and pears, I am allergic to fruit* is a complex sentence. Notice that the idea of liking peaches and pears is subordinated to the idea of being allergic to fruit. Thus, the writer has emphasized the second idea, making it the more important of the two ideas.

- A **compound-complex** sentence has two or more principal clauses and one or more subordinate clauses. *Although I like peaches and pears, I am allergic to fruit and I try to avoid eating any* is a compound-complex sentence. The writer uses this kind of sentence to imply that "I am allergic to fruit" and "I try to avoid eating any" are of equal importance, but more important that "I like peaches and pears".

- A good essay will have a variety of sentence structures. In addition, the kind of structure which the writer chooses tells the reader what the writer considers to be important. This technique of subordination is discussed further in part (g).

EDITING AND REVISING (Continued)

2. STYLE (Continued):

b) Precise and Effective Diction:

We have all heard people say, "Well, you know what I mean" when they are unable to express their ideas clearly. In addition, we all have difficulty expressing ourselves at certain times. When we speak, we do not have a great deal of time to choose the exact word to express our meaning. When we write, however, and particularly when we edit and revise our writing, we do have the time to choose the most effective works. *Diction* refers to our choice of language, the words we use to express our ideas.

Following are some ways to use language more precisely and effectively:

- **Use words for their precise meanings.** There are several words which students misuse; learning the precise use of these words can improve the tone of an essay

  - **a lot**: A lot is a parcel of land. A writer who is referring to quantity should use expressions such as *many, much, or a great deal. Many students attended the party* has a more formal tone than *A lot of students attended the party.* Similarly, *a great deal of money* is more formal than *a lot of money.*

  - **just**: This word means *fair* or *honest.* She was *just seventeen* is acceptable in speech, but *She was only seventeen* is more appropriate in formal writing.

  - **disinterested**: This word means *fair* or *impartial.* It does not mean *uninterested.* One would expect a judge at a trial to be *disinterested* but would be upset if the judge were *uninterested.*

  - **affect, effect**: *Affect* is a verb; *effect* is generally a noun (except in the expression to *effect a change* which means *to bring about). The novel had a major effect on my life* (noun). *The novel affected me greatly* (verb).

  - **accept, except**: *Accept* is a verb meaning *to receive. Except* is a preposition meaning *not including. Except* may be used as a verb to mean *exclude.*

  - **aggravate**: *Aggravate* means *make worse,* as in *His health problem was aggravated by lack of money.* It does not mean *irritate* or *annoy.*

  - **imply, infer**: *To imply* is *to insinuate;* to *infer* is *to draw a conclusion.* Thus, the writer or speaker *implies;* the reader or listener *infers.*

  - **lead, led**: *Led* is the past tense of the verb, *lead. Lead* when pronounced led refers to the metal.

These are only some examples of words which are often used imprecisely.

EDITING AND REVISING (Continued)

2. STYLE (Continued):

b) Precise and Effective Diction (Continued):

- Avoid a general word when a specific word is possible: Sometimes when we cannot think of the exact word, we use general words. When students revise their writing, they should look out for general words and whenever possible substitute specific words for them. Some examples of general words are *thing, man, person, idea.* Using specific nouns and verbs will be discussed in part (c).

- Avoid clichés and trite expressions: A cliché is an overworked expression which has been used so much that readers are tired of hearing it. Some examples are: *and now without further ado, like a bolt from the blue, naked eye, slowly but surely, drastic action, quiet as a mouse, raining cats and dogs.*

- Using figurative language: Metaphors, similes and other comparisons can create vivid pictures in the reader's mind. Unlike clichés, original figurative language can allow the writer to make a point more clearly. *Like a mouse trapped by a cat, Brutus cannot win against the superior political skills of Antony* is an example of figurative language which can arouse the reader's interest. Occasional use of figurative language adds an element of artistry to writing.

- Avoid gobbledygook and pretentious diction: Often the simplest way of saying something is the most effective. Gobbledygook is expressing something simple in a complicated way, such as saying *lacteal fluid for milk.* Some writers wish to sound intellectual so they may use what students often call "big words" or *pretentious diction;* some may even go so far as to look for "bigger" words in a thesaurus. Writers need to sound natural and honest, but they need also to take into account the audience, as pointed out in part (d). A natural, honest effect can be achieved if writers use language which is comfortable for both themselves and their readers.

c) Precise and Effective Nouns and Verbs:

A writer who chooses specific rather than general words will communicate most effectively. Writers should examine the nouns and verbs which they use in writing to see if more specific words can be used. A sentence like *The man walked into the room* does communicate an idea, but it is a very general one. *The drunk stumbled into the salon* uses two specific nouns and a specific verb to communicate a much clearer picture. *The waiter waltzed into the kitchen* offers another clear picture. Note that the latter two examples essentially say *The man walked into the room,* but they also say much more.

It is a worthwhile activity for students to go through a piece of writing underlining each time the verb *to be* is used, as *is, are, was* and *were.* Many writers over-use the verb *to be* and other copula verbs such as *seem, feel* or *look,* which are not very specific. Often these verbs can be replaced by others which are most precise.

EDITING AND REVISING (Continued)

d) The Intended Audience:

A writer must choose words that he or she feels comfortable with; however, the writer must also choose language appropriate to the intended audience of the piece of writing. If the intended is a child, the writer will normally use fairly simple vocabulary. The intended audience of most essays, however, is a secondary school teacher or university professor. The writer, therefore, needs to use vocabulary which will make the reader feel comfortable. This does not mean that the writer should use pretentious language, but the essay does require a degree of formality and an avoidance of slang or colloquialisms in most cases. Slang or colloquial language may, however, be appropriate if the writer is aiming for a particular effect; the writer, of course, is the final decision-maker.

e) Tone:

Just as the tone of voice of a speaker suggests his or her attitude, so written language also has a **tone**. Tone in writing is the attitude the writer takes towards the subject matter and the audience. It may be serious or humorous, sincere or detached, sarcastic or ironic, conversational or formal, and so on. The tone of a piece of writing creates a sound or impression. Thus, the writer of an essay has to be sure to choose a tone which is appropriate to the particular piece of writing and to the reader of that piece.

f) Focus and Emphasis:

The arrangement of words in a sentence is important for emphasis. The subject of the sentence is normally the most important idea in a sentence, and this is called the **focus**. What the subject is doing is the **emphasis**. Careless writers often use a less important idea as the subject of a sentence, and such a sentence will, therefore, lack focus. The most _common example is a sentence such as the following: In William Shakespeare's play, Julius_ Caesar, _he portrays Brutus as a man to be admired._ As it is written, the subject of this sentence is the pronoun _he_, a word which refers to William Shakespeare. But the writer _must determine the focus of this sentence. A revision such as, In his play, Julius Caesar,_ William Shakespeare portrays Brutus as a man to be admired, shifts the focus to William Shakespeare, and this sentence is stronger than the first one. However, if the proposition of the essay is _Brutus is a man to be admired_, then _Brutus_ and not Shakespeare should be the _focus. The strongest sentence will read, In William Shakespeare's play, Julius Caesar,_ _Brutus is a man to be admired._ Here the focus is clearly _Brutus_ and the emphasis is _is a_ man to be admired. Note that the original sentence stated that the focus was _he_ and the emphasis was _portrayed_. The third sentence is clearly the most effective one because it emphasizes what the writer believes is important.

Focus and emphasis are skills developed by a mature writer. Teachers should not expect students to master them instantly. However, teachers should expose students to the concept and reinforce it over subsequent years.

EDITING AND REVISING (Continued)

2. STYLE (Continued):

g) Subordination:

As a writer learns focus and emphasis, so he or she should also learn about subordination. This technique was touched on in the section on **Sentence Variation** on page 30. **Subordination** means that the most important ideas in a sentence are placed in principal clauses and the lesser ideas are placed in subordinate clauses:

- *Jennifer ate lunch and then she took her brother to the park.* This sentence contains two principal clauses, *Jennifer ate lunch* and *she took her brother to the park.* By choosing to use two principal clauses, the writer is saying that both of these ideas are of equal value.

- *After Jennifer ate lunch, she took her brother to the park.* This sentence contains a principal clause, *she took her brother to the park*, and a subordinate clause, *after Jennifer ate lunch.* By arranging the sentence in this way, the writer is saying that taking her brother to the park is more important than Jennifer's eating lunch.

- *Jennifer ate lunch before she took her brother to the park.* This sentence reverses the subordination, and therefore emphasizes Jennifer's eating lunch.

Thus, by using the technique of subordination, the writer can choose to emphasize what he or she feels is important.

h) Parallel Structure:

Speakers like John F. Kennedy and Martin Luther King made very successful use of a technique called parallel structure. **Parallel structure** is the repetition of a grammatical structure:

- *Alphonse is handsome, wealthy and has graduated from college.* This sentence lacks parallel structure since the words *handsome* and *wealthy* are single adjectives (and are therefore parallel), but the expression *has graduated from college* is a principal clause. The writer needs to change it to a single adjective, such as *educated. Alphonse is handsome, wealthy and educated* shows good parallel structure, is more coherent to read, and (as students often say) sounds better.

EDITING AND REVISING (Continued)

2. STYLE (Continued):

h) Parallel Structure (Continued):

- *Exercising every day, eat nutritiously and having a regular physical examination can lead to a healthy life.* Again the parallel structure can be achieved by repeating the grammatical structure of the gerund, *exercising.* *Exercising every day, eating nutritiously and having a regular physical examination can lead to a healthy life* retains the parallelism.

- Expressions like *both...and* or *not only...but also* can create problems with parellelism. *Amanda both corrected my spelling and she typed my essay* lacks parallel structure. The grammatical structure of the words following *both* should be the same as the grammatical structure of the words following *and.* Clearly, *corrected my spelling* and *she typed my essay* are not grammatically parallel. In this case, the correction is simple: *Amanda both corrected my spelling and typed my essay.* A similar problem occurs in the following sentence: *Peter was not only a good student but also he showed skill in athletics.* *A good student* consists of an article (*a*), an adjective (*good*) and a noun (*student*); what follows but also consists of a clause with a subjective (*he*) and a verb (*showed*) with other words added. Again the change is simple: *Peter was not only a good student but also an excellent athlete.*

- *The refrigerator, weighing 800 pounds, and which two men could hardly carry, was delivered to our house.* This sentence contains a participial phrase and an adjective clause. By replacing the phrase with an adjective clause, the writer can achieve parallel structure: *The refrigerator, which weighed 800 pounds and which two men could hardly carry, was delivered to our house.*

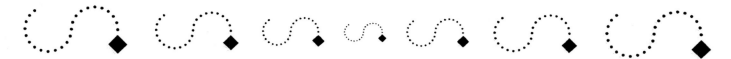
2. STYLE (Continued):

i) Varying Syntax:

The arrangement of words to form a sentence is called **syntax**. Many unsophisticated writers begin each sentence with the subject and follow it with the verb. This kind of writing is dull. Varying the syntax or the arrangement of the words leads to writing which is more interesting to read. Each sentence in the following paragraph begins with the subject, followed by the verb. Note how dull it sounds:

- Young Charles Dickens was no stranger to poverty. His father was a poorly paid civil servant who was forced to move his family from place to place. Dickens developed a fascination with ships in Portsmouth which would provide material for his later novels, including <u>Great Expectations</u>. The family moved later to Chatham, Kent, an area, which would be the basis for the marsh country of <u>Great Expectations</u>. The family moved to London when Charles was about ten years old. Charles's father was sent to debtors' prison. Charles, the second oldest of eight children, was forced to find work in a factory, labeling pots of blacking, a substance used for restoring the shiny black color to fireplace grates.

When the syntax is varied (that is, when each sentence does not being with the subject followed by the verb), the writing is much more interesting:

- Young Charles Dickens was no stranger to poverty. A poorly paid civil servant, his father was forced to move his family from place to place. In Portsmouth, Dickens developed a fascination with ships which would provide material for his later novels, including <u>Great Expectations</u>. Later, the family moved to Chatham, Kent, an area which would be the basis for the marsh country of <u>Great Expectations</u>. When Charles was about ten years old, the family moved to London. Charles's father was sent to debtors' prison. The second oldest of eight children, Charles was forced to find work in a factory, labeling pots of blacking, a substance used for restoring the shiny black color to fireplace grates.

There are many more elements of style which are not included in this unit. Students who have mastered the topics included here may consult any of the works included in the resource section.

EDITING AND REVISING (Continued)

3. ACTIVITIES TO IMPROVE STYLE:

A student who is beginning to learn to write an essay needs to work on content and organization; mechanics such as correct spelling and grammar have been learned since the student started to speak and write.

Style is the polishing technique of essay-writing and is an important focus in the senior grades of high school and at the college or university level.

Teachers should not expect all students to accomplish all of the following activities in their first year of essay writing. These activities are designed for students as they mature through the essay writing process and may be used over the ensuing years.

EDITING AND REVISING (Continued)

3. ACTIVITIES TO IMPROVE STYLE:

a) Sentence Variation:

1. This exercise may be performed individually by students or done in by small groups, each group working on a different task.

    Following are a list of ideas which can be combined to make one or more sentences.

    Form sentences from the ideas in order to create each of the following effects.

    a) the effect of speed
    b) a loose sentence
    c) a periodic sentence
    d) a series of sentences which vary in length
    e) a series of sentences which are all simple sentences or all compound sentences
    f) a series of sentences which vary in structure (simple, compound, complex, etc.)

Here are the ideas to combine:

> Brutus is an honorable person
> Brutus has a good reputation in Rome
> Even Marc Antony respects Brutus
> Antony says that Brutus is "the noblest Roman of them all"
> Cassius wants Brutus in the conspiracy
> Cassius thinks Brutus's reputation will help the cause.

2. In pairs or groups of three, combine the following sentences into a four-sentence paragraph. Include all the major ideas. Use a variety of sentence lengths and a variety of sentence structures.

    Charles Dickens was born on February 7, 1812. He was born in Portsmouth. Portsmouth is a sea-port on the south coast of England. Dickens developed a fascination with ships. He used his love of ships in some of his novels. When Dickens was ten, his family moved to London. They experienced great financial difficulties. His father was sent to debtors' prison. Charles was the second oldest of eight children. He was forced to find work. He worked in a blacking factory. Blacking is used to restore the shiny, black color to fireplaces. Charles's job was labeling jars. He also used this experience in his books.

EDITING AND REVISING (Continued)

3. ACTIVITIES TO IMIPROVE STYLE (Continued):

b) Precise and Effective Diction:

1. Some of the following sentences contain errors in the misuse of words. The student's task is to determine what words are used incorrectly and to correct them. Although many of the words are taken from the list on page 32, not all these words are used incorrectly. There are also errors in the use of words not found on page 32.

   a) I am just trying to say that what you inferred is wrong.
   b) Please accept my apology for aggravating you this morning.
   c) The athlete's illness affected her performance in the race and her poor showing lead to her disqualification.
   d) A lot of students enjoy alternative music just because they accept anything that their peers like.
   e) Marnie likes all fish except shrimp which aggravate her allergies.
   f) In order to resolve their dispute, the two sides have called in a disinterested person to arbitrate.
   g) I don't mean to infer that I am disinterested in sports; actually, exercise effects my respiratory system.
   h) The school principal is a woman whose concern for students lead to her promotion.

2. Make a list of five specific words which might replace the italicized word in each of the following sentences:

   a) Hand me the *thing* on the desk.
   b) The *man* knocked on our door.
   c) Maia is a *nice* person.
   d) In the still night, we heard a *sound*..
   e) The artist could *do good stuff.*
   f) When Odelia looked at the picture, she felt *funny*.

3. Complete each of the following ideas with a creative, original metaphor or simile:

   a) Love is like....
   b) The leader of our country should be a....
   c) Ben moved along the path like a....
   d) Judy avoids work like a....
   e) Writing an essay is like....

EDITING AND REVISING (Continued)

3. ACTIVITIES TO IMPROVE STYLE (Continued):

b) Precise and Effective Diction (Continued):

4. Rewrite each of the following sentences by replacing clichés, gobbledygook or pretentious words with more creative expressions.

   a) Slowly but surely, the weary travelers wended their way home.

   b) The aqueous substance in the glass was indubitably colored green.

   c) Last but by no means least is a man who has given his all to the team.

   d) In our world today everyday people can become the proud possessors of new places of habitation.

   e) The idea struck Jason like a bolt from the blue.

   f) As my better half would say, "You have to stay abreast of the times."

   g) Allyson was scared to death by the specimen of humanity she saw before her.

   h) It is not at all feasible to proceed down the path that you have chosen.

   i) In the wee, small hours of the morning, Brent breathed a sigh of relief that he had not been proscripted into the armed forces.

   j) Any team that endeavors to unseat our victorious Trojans will be doomed to disappointment.

5. Write the ugliest, most awful sentence you can think of, filled with clichés, trite expressions, gobbledygook and pretentious diction. Share your sentence with your classmates.

c) Precise and Effective Nouns and Verbs:

1. Make a list of five words or expressions to replace the italicized word or words in each of the following sentences. Be sure that your replacements are very specific words.

   a) The *man walked* into the *room*.

   b) The *leader said* she would consider the *matter*.

   c) *A person was* in front of the *building*.

   d) The *animal called* to its mate.

   e) *She moved* slowly down the *road*.

EDITING AND REVISING (Continued)

3. ACTIVITIES TO IMPROVE STYLE (Continued):

d) The Intended Audience:

1. Decide what you most want to do in life: What is your major goal? In two or three sentences for each one describe this goal using language appropriate for:

    a) an audience of children

    b) a resume for a job

    c) an audience of your closest friends.

    d) one of the following: the President of the United States, the Prime Minister of Canada, an international religious leader, or any person of international stature

    e) your favorite singer, musician or athlete

e) Tone:

1. Repeat the exercise in *Part (d) Intended Audience* using any of the following tones: humorous, sarcastic or ironic, sincere, condescending, angry.

f) Focus and Emphasis:

1. Each of the following sentences contains a weak focus and therefore the wrong emphasis. Rewrite each sentence with a clear focus and emphasis.

    a) In <u>Great Expectations</u> by Charles Dickens, he presents a central character named Pip whose personality changes drastically as the novel progresses.

    b) There are many different causes of World War I.

    c) In this essay it has been shown that Brutus is a character worthy of the admiration of the audience.

    d) It's very difficult to drive a car well.

    e) It seems as if Brutus can be easily manipulated by characters like Cassius and Antony.

    f) In examining the character of Romeo, the reader can see that his actions, not fate or any other outside forces, cause his downfall.

    g) <u>Huckleberry Finn</u> is a novel about a good-hearted boy in a hypocritical world. This is why the book is so popular.

    h) The movie has several characters who try to find romance but find only unhappiness instead.

EDITING AND REVISING (Continued)

3. ACTIVITIES TO IMPROVE STYLE (Continued):

f) Focus and Emphasis (Continued):

   i) Looking down the road you can see the lights of the city and the buildings silhouetted against the night sky.

   j) Canada promised British Columbia that a railway would be built across the country. That is the reason British Columbia joined the Canadian confederation.

g) Subordination:

1. Combine each of the following sets of sentences into one sentence. Decide which idea is more important and place this idea in the principal clause. Subordinate the less important idea.

   a) Joshua hit Katherine. Katherine told her parents.

   b) Julius Caesar is the title character in the play. He is an arrogant and short-sighted leader.

   c) Hong Kong and Macau were once colonies of Great Britain and Portugal. Soon they will be part of China.

   d) Jamal went shopping at the Eaton Center. He bought a new bathing suit and sandals.

   e) To Kill A Mockingbird is Harper Lee's only novel. It has sold millions of copies and has been made into a successful movie.

   f) Our flight to London passed over Greenland. Greenland looks very snowy and icy from the sky.

   g) George Washington is known as the father of his country. He was the first President of the United States.

   h) Beauty and the Beast was very successful at movie theaters and on videotape. It was also successful as a Broadway musical.

   i) Luke spent about two hours doing his Algebra homework. Then he talked to Tara for two hours on the telephone.

   j) Luigi makes an excellent double cheese and mushroom pizza. He owns one of the most popular new restaurants in the city.

h) Parallel Structure:

1. Each of the following sentences contains one or more errors in parallel structure. Determine the error in each case. Then rewrite the sentence to correct the error.

   a) Last month was my first attempt at writing an essay and needed a great deal of revision.

EDITING AND REVISING (Continued)

3. ACTIVITIES TO IMPROVE STYLE (Continued):

h) Parallel Structure (Continued):

b) The constitution of the newly independent Caribbean island granted all citizens the right to freedom of religion, to publish their ideas in newspapers and adequate housing.

c) Among the immigrants to America, the Poles worked hard, learned to speak English and their children were well educated.

d) Kirsten was not only a good athlete but she also excelled in acting.

e) Brutus was a good leader, wise husband, and he had the respect of the people of Rome.

f) Sherlock Holmes solved each mystery either by questioning the people involved or he used logical deduction.

g) Margaret Laurence is an author who has written several novels and she has written many short stories.

h) When we consider its beautiful parks, when we walk its safe streets and it has good entertainment facilities, we see that Los Angeles is a good place to live.

i) When Pip first met Estella in Great Expectations, he knew he was in love and she would be the only girl for him.

j) Three ways to achieve good style are using parallel structure, subordinate less important ideas, and precise nouns.

i) Varying Syntax:

1. The following paragraph contains sentences which all begin with the subject followed by the verb. Rewrite the paragraph varying the syntax:

Brutus is well-respected by all the citizens of Rome. Cassius says of him, "Well, Brutus, thou art noble." Cassius wants Brutus to join the conspiracy against Julius Caesar because the citizens of Rome will respect Brutus. This noble aspect of the character of Brutus is echoed by others in the play. The Third Citizen says, "The noble Brutus is ascended", when Brutus begins to speak at Caesar's funeral. The citizen says this even though all the crowd are angry because Brutus has killed Caesar. Ligarius respects Brutus so much that he says he will arise from his sick-bed if Brutus desires it: "I am not sick if Brutus have in hand/Any exploit worthy the name of honor." These traits of nobility and honor are also presented by Antony in his funeral oration. Antony refers to "the noble Brutus" and says, "Brutus is an honorable man." Antony repeats these thoughts at the end of the play when he refers to Brutus as "the noblest Roman of them all." It is clear then that Brutus is well-respected by the Romans.

EDITING AND REVISING (Continued)

4. MECHANICS:

Not all students have the same problems with essay-writing mechanics. Some are good spellers, others are not. Some have problems with grammar, others have not. Therefore, students need to determine their areas of difficulty and work on these specific areas.

This resource deals only with some of the problem areas of mechanics; it is not possible to deal with every difficulty. In addition, there are many good reference books available to students who need them.

Therefore, this section covers only some of the most widespread problem areas. These are:

a) common errors in spelling

b) consistent verb tense

c) the use of the apostrophe

d) agreement of pronouns with their antecedents

e) the use of the semicolon.

EDITING AND REVISING (Continued)

4. MECHANICS (Continued):

a) Common Errors in Spelling:

Many students have no difficulty in spelling and are able to see their errors clearly when they edit their writing. Others have a great deal of difficulty. There are, however, words which students consistently misspell and students need to be aware of these. A writer can easily improve spelling if he or she is on the lookout for specific words which cause problems.

Following is a list of words that appear incorrectly spelled in many students' writing:

- **receive**: The *"i" before "e"* rule has too many exceptions to be considered a rule. Generally, *"ei"* will follow the letter *"c"*, and students need to bear this in mind when writing words like **receive, deceive, conceive, ceiling**.

- **achieve**: There are many words which follow the rule such as: **achieve, friend, piece, chief** and **relieve**.

- **separate**: Note that the letter *"a"* follows the *"p"*.

- **definite**: Note *"ite"*, not *"ate"*.

- **their, they're, there**: **Their** is possessive, meaning "belonging to them". **They're** is the contraction for "there are". **There** means "in that place".

- **occurred, occurring, referred, referring, preferred, preferring**: These words double the letter *"r"* before adding *"ed"* or *"ing"*. Note also **occurrence** doubles the *"r"*, but **reference** and **preference** do not.

- **dependent, independent**: These adjectives are spelled *"ent"*. **Dependent** with an *"a"* is a noun often seen on income tax forms to mean "someone who is dependent".

- **words beginning with a prefix such as "un", "re" or "mis"**: Simply add the prefix to the word, as in **unnecessary, recommend** or **misspell**.

Activity on Spelling:

Create your own **spelling collage**, using a piece of bristol board. Make a list of words you misspell. When a word appears on the list three times, put it on the bristol board collage.

EDITING AND REVISING (Continued)

4. MECHANICS (Continued):

b) Consistent Verb Tense:

It is an accepted rule or convention among essay writers to use one verb tense throughout the essay. If the writer begins in the present tense, he or she should not switch to past tense, but should keep the present tense for the entire essay. Alternatively, the writer may choose to use the past tense throughout the essay. Either tense is acceptable.

It is logical for the writer to keep to one tense. Since verb tenses represent time, the implication is that an activity done in the past happened before one done in the present. Thus, since the writer often does not wish to show this time relationship, he or she uses one consistent verb tense throughout an essay.

Sometimes students have problems when they write an essay in the present tense, but a quotation which they cite uses the past tense. In this case, the tense of the quotation should remain unchanged. Here is an example:

- In A Tale of Two Cities, Charles Dickens provides the setting in the first paragraph when he states, "It was the best of times, it was the worst of times."

Again by convention, writers would not see this switch in verb tense as a problem.

Students need to edit each essay looking for consistent verb tense. It is worth the extra effort because it results in more mature writing.

Activity on Consistent Verb Tense:

Rewrite the following paragraph using a consistent verb tense:

Julius Caesar was one of the most arrogant of Rome's leaders. He shows his arrogance when he announces his wife's inability to conceive children in public at the races in the second scene of the play. He also showed it when he refuses to listen to the Soothsayer who told him, "Beware the Ides of March." Caesar later answered, "The Ides of March are come", as if he is challenging fate. He seemed to think that somehow he could not be hurt because he is such a special human being.

4. MECHANICS (Continued):

c) The Use of the Apostrophe:

Some students have difficulty using the apostrophe correctly. The rules which follow are very simple. Many writers try to complicate these rules by making exceptions to them, but these rules can cover every major example of the apostrophe.

Uses of the Apostrophe:

- Possession in nouns
- Contractions

The apostrophe is used to show **possession** or **ownership**. Originally possession was shown in Anglo-Saxon by the addition of the letters *"es"* to a noun. The *"e"* was later omitted and the apostrophe was used in its place.

The apostrophe is also used to show the omission of letters in **contractions**. Contractions are two words shortened into one word by omitting letters. Some common contractions are *didn't* (the letter *"o"* is omitted), *who's* (meaning *who is*), *they're* (meaning *they are*).

Using the Apostrophe to Form Possession:

Singular nouns form possession by adding *'s* to the noun. Follow this rule and you will always be correct, even if the noun end in *s*. Some examples:

- Boy = singular noun   boy's = belonging to the boy
- Mr. Smith = singular noun   Mr. Smith's = belonging to Mr. Smith
- Brutus = singular noun   Brutus's = belonging to Brutus
- Dickens = singular noun   Dickens's = belonging to Dickens

Plural nouns ending in *s* form possession by adding *'* to the noun. Some examples:

- Boys – plural noun   boys' = belonging to the boys

Plural nouns not ending in *s* form possession by adding *'s* to the noun. Examples:

- Children = plural noun   children's = belonging to the children
- Data = plural noun   data's = belonging to the data
- Women = plural noun   women's = belonging to the women

EDITING AND REVISING (Continued)

4. MECHANICS (Continued):

c) The Use of the Apostrophe (Continued):

Writers who follow the rules on page 48 will **never be wrong** in forming possession. There are writers and grammarians who complicate these rules by saying that if the singular noun ending in *s* is pronounced *es* then one adds *'s*; if the word is not pronounced *es* then add only the apostrophe; *Jesus' sake* (meaning for the sake of Jesus) would then be pronounced *Jesus sake*, but *Jesus's sake* would be pronounced Jesuses sake. This kind of usage is often found in hymns or prayers using poetry, but for most practical purposes it unnecessarily complicates a simple rule of the English language (and really there are not very many simple rules that apply, are there? So why complicate it?)

Using the Apostrophe with Pronouns:

The apostrophe is **never used with personal pronouns to form possession**; it is used only to form **contractions**. Here are some examples:

- *Who's* = who is; the possessive is *whose*
- *Their's* does not exist; the possessive is *theirs*
- *Our's* similarly does not exist; the possessive is *ours*

Indefinite pronouns, however, **use the apostrophe to form possession**. Indefinite pronouns are words like *one, everyone, anyone, etc.* Here are some examples:

- Everyone's job
- One's own work.

These simple rules will govern the use of the apostrophe. Many students have difficulty with the concept because they either confuse the meaning of the term *possession* or they are overwhelmed by the number of seeming exceptions. If the teacher stresses that there are no exceptions, then the task becomes easier for students to learn.

4. MECHANICS (Continued):

c) The Use of the Apostrophe (Continued):

Activity on the use of the Apostrophe:

1. Form the possessive of each of the following words:

   a) John
   b) Athlete
   c) John Keats
   d) United States
   e) United States of America
   f) India
   g) Potatoes
   h) Donovan Bailey
   i) Sisters
   j) Mississippi

2. Four words in the following sentences contain incorrect apostrophes. Four other words are missing required apostrophes. In groups of two or three, decide which are the four incorrect words and which four words need apostrophes. Be prepared to support your answers.

   In his works Dicken's often writes about the evils of society. He knows about debtors prison because his father spent some time in a prison. He knows also about the evils' of the workhouse, where people who are very poor have to live in order to eat. Oliver Twist is a character who's life begins in a workhouse, but Oliver is adopted by a rich family. However, Dickens does not believe that life is easy. Oliver is kidnapped by Fagin and his boys who are pickpockets. The boys steal from people but they aren't sorry for it. The pickpockets' job is really to support Fagins lifestyle by providing him with articles he may sell. An acquaintance of Fagin named Nancy tells Olivers new parents where they can find him, but Nancy's boyfriend, Bill Sykes, kills' her. Finally, Fagin and Bill Sykes are punished for their crimes. Dickens novel, <u>Oliver Twist</u>, clearly shows problems in society.

EDITING AND REVISING (Continued)

4. MECHANICS (Continued):

d) Agreement of Pronouns with their Antecedents:

There are several pronouns which present problems for students in essay writing. Sometimes, the problem is caused by a gender issue: The English language has very few pronouns which are not gender specific; those few that are (as indicated below) often require a gender specific pronoun.

Words like **everyone, one, anyone, someone, every, each**, and additional words like **a person, a writer, a student**, are **singular** and must have **singular pronouns** following them. Here is an example:

- **Everyone in the class will do his or her best.** Since the word *everyone* is singular, it requires a singular pronoun to follow it. The English language does not have a word which covers both male and female, so the writer is doomed to the *his or her* technique of writing. Note that the use of a plural phrase such as **All the students** would take a plural pronoun: **All students will do their best.**

A similar situation occurs with the use of a phrase like "a person". Again, "a person" is singular, not plural, and so requires a singular pronoun following it:

- **If a person does his or her best, he or she will benefit from the results.** Obviously this phrase is awkward, but it is grammatically correct. This kind of awkwardness can be avoided by avoiding the singular "a person".

- **If all do their best, they will benefit from the results.** This sentence avoids the awkwardness.

Activity on Pronoun and Antecedent:

1. In the space provided write the correct pronoun. Then rewrite the sentence using a plural pronoun and plural antecedent.

   a) Every person expects a great deal of help from _____ friends.

   b) A person expects a great deal of help from _____ friends.

   c) When Donovan Bailey spoke to the interviewer he was always respectful to _____.

   d) Everyone in the class will try _____ hardest to pass the examination.

   e) Brutus is someone who always considers _____ wife's feelings.

EDITING AND REVISING (Continued)

4. MECHANICS (Continued):

e) The Use of the Semicolon:

Using the semicolon correctly is one of the marks of the sophisticated writer. Yet, the semicolon is very easy to use. Only two rules govern its usage; the first rule, however, has two parts to it:

The soft period rule: Use a semicolon to separate two closely related sentences:

- There were several causes of World War I; the most important of these is the assassination of the Archduke Franz Ferdinand. These two sentences could be written with a period between them. However, they are so closely related that a semicolon replaces the period. Note that they could be written as one sentence: **Of all the causes of the First World War, the most important is the assassination of the Archduke Franz Ferdinand.**

Use a semicolon to separate two sentences if the second sentence begins with an introductory expression such as *however, moreover, for example, for instance, nevertheless, namely, for instance, etc.*

- Brutus is a friend of Julius Caesar; nevertheless, he joins the conspiracy to kill him. Again the two sentences are closely related. The introductory word *nevertheless* is preceded by a semicolon and followed by a comma.

- Brutus is a friend of Julius Caesar. Nevertheless, he joins the conspiracy to kill him. The period here separates the two sentences; the semicolon suggests their close relationship.

- Brutus is a friend of Julius Caesar; however, he joins the conspiracy to kill him. Note that this sentence is the same as the first example.

- Brutus, however, is a friend of Julius Caesar. Note that the word *however* is set off in commas; there is no semicolon because there is no separate sentence.

EDITING AND REVISING (Conitinued)

4. MECHANICS (Continued):

e) The Use of the Semicolon (Continued):

The hard comma rule: Use a semicolon between co-ordinate parts of a sentence which have commas between them. Here the semicolon separates parts that would otherwise be confused.

- The people invited to the party were Mary her sister Rose her mother and her aunt. How many people were invited to the party? There could be up to five. Check the differences in the following sentences:

- The people invited to the party were Mary, her sister, Rose, her mother, and her aunt. This sentence indicates that five people were invited.

- The people invited to the party were Mary; her sister, Rose; her mother; and her aunt. This sentence indicates that four people were invited and also tells the reader that Rose is Mary's sister.

- The people invited to the party were Mary; her sister; Rose, her mother; and her aunt. Again four people were invited, but now Rose is her mother.

- The people invited to the party were Mary, her sister; Rose, her mother; and her aunt. Now three people were invited and Mary is the sister of the hostess. Note that the semicolon allows the writer to express an exact meaning which would otherwise be lost.

Activity on the Use of the Semicolon:

1. Check through your essay. Find where you can use a semicolon. Look particularly for a sentence which begins with **for example**. Place a semicolon before **for example** and a comma after it. Be sure that what follows *for example* is a complete sentence. If it is not a complete sentence, use commas before and after *for example*.

EDITING AND REVISING (Continued)

5. CONCLUSION:

Often people say after they have been asked a question, "I wish I had had time to think about my answer before I spoke." When students write an essay, they have time to think before they write. That is why the revision process is so helpful in any successful writing. D.H. Lawrence rewrote <u>Sons and Lovers</u> seven times before he submitted it for publication, and even then he was not completely satisfied.

Professional writers know the advantages of the revision process. Students need to learn these same advantages. For this reason, this section called "Editing and Revising" has taken such a large part of this resource.

Editing is not merely proofreading. It is a meaningful part of the writing process and teachers need to provide the classroom time it deserves. If a student peer-edits another student's writing and simply writes the comment, "Good work", then either the student is lazy or he/she does not know how to peer-edit. Working through this unit should give the student the tools necessary to do the job properly.

WRITING THE FINAL DRAFT

If a student has followed all the steps in this unit, writing the final draft of the essay will be simple, because all the work has been done. A student who wrote the first draft on a word-processor has been able to make revisions quite simply. Now all that needs to be done is to put the program through spell-check and format it to fit the pages.

What follows is a checklist for the final copy of the essay:

- Be sure that the essay is doubled-spaced and the adequate margins have been left on all sides.

- Use the accepted format for footnotes and bibliography.

- Ensure that quotations are incorporated properly into the essay.

- Add a title page.

- Some teachers like students to put their essays into duotangs because these add a touch of formality to the assignment; other teachers do not like duotangs because they add more bulk. Since the teacher has to carry the essays home or to another room to begin the arduous job of marking, he or she may resent the added bulk caused by the duotangs. As with everything else essay writing, the student should check with the teacher before submitting the essay.

- Proofread the essay carefully. Even a good spell-check program will not be able to catch typographical errors.

A SAMPLE ESSAY

What follows in the next few pages is a sample essay on the novel, Great Expectations, by Charles Dickens.

It follows the pattern taught in this book and is intended to be fairly typical grade eleven essay. Of course, a student in the higher grades should be capable of writing an essay which is better than this one.

This sample essay, therefore, is a good model for students who are learning to write an essay.

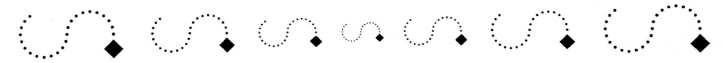

A SAMPLE ESSAY

THE ENDINGS OF <u>GREAT EXPECTATIONS</u>

Although in life things often end sadly, readers of novels are conditioned to expect happy endings. Thus, in writing the relatively unhappy <u>Great Expectations</u>, Charles Dickens faced a dilemma. Originally, the novel ended logically but unhappily with Pip and Estella remaining forever apart. However, Dickens's reading public objected and the author rewrote the ending of the novel. The original ending, however, is more effective that the rewritten ending. Estella cannot possibly change enough to ensure the success of the happy marriage to Pip which is implied in the rewritten ending. Similarly, the entire focus of the novel, including its theme and purpose, is directed towards the final separation of Estella and Pip. For these reasons, the original ending of <u>Great Expectations</u> is the more effective ending.

The original ending is more effective because Estella is not capable of the change in character which would be necessary if she and Pip were to marry and live happily together. Estella has already admitted to Pip that she has no heart:

> "Oh! I have a heart to be stabbed in or shot in, I have no doubt," said Estella, "and, of course, if it ceased to beat I should cease to be. But you know what I mean. I have no softness there, no -- sympathy -- sentiment -- nonsense."[1]

---

[1]Charles Dickens, <u>Great Expectations</u>, (New York: The Macmillan Company Limited, 1965), p.236.

A SAMPLE ESSAY (pg. 2)

Estella proves her heartlessness many times in the novel primarily through her callous treatment of Pip and her vindictive nature even towards Miss Havisham to whom she also cannot show any real affection:

> Mother by adoption, I have said that I owe everything to you.
> All I possess is freely yours. All that you have given me is at your
> command to have again. Beyond that, I have nothing. And if
> you ask me to give you what you never gave me, my gratitude
> and duty cannot do impossibilities.[2]

Estella freely admits that she cannot be anything but what she is. In fact, her marriage to the sulky and rude Bentley Drummle is the final insult to Pip. She can not possibly change sufficiently to make Pip a loving and faithful wife as the rewritten ending implies, and, therefore, the original ending is the more effective one.

In addition, Estella's inability to change her character is part of the original focus of a novel which leads logically and directly to the first ending. Great Expectations is a novel whose theme is the corruption of the individual by undeserved expectation. Pip is corrupted by Magwitch's money which has neither earned nor deserved, and he learns through work and suffering that it is foolish to live in a world where he deludes himself with false hopes of being an idle gentleman. This he in fact does learn, though suffering in helping Magwitch and working for eleven years. For Pip simply to come home and start

---

[2]Ibid., p. 304.

A SAMPLE ESSAY (pg. 3)

again where he left off would mean that there is no real purpose to the novel. The reader has grown with Pip through 58 chapters of the novel to the point when Pip shows that he has learned his lesson in chapter 59 in the original ending:

> For in her face, and in her voice, and in her touch, she gave
> me the assurance that suffering had been stronger than Miss
> Havisham's teaching, and had given her a heart to understand
> what my heart used to be.[3]

It is this lesson which the novel aims at and Pip's reward is the knowledge that one benefits in life through hard work, not through childish wish-fulfillment. Since only the original ending can reinforce Dickens's purpose, which is after all the entire focus of the novel, then it is clear that the original ending is the more effective one.

The dual endings of Great Expectations have provoked a great deal of controversy. However, since Estella cannot realistically complete the change in character required by the rewritten ending, and since the original ending so substantially reinforces the focus of the novel, the original ending must be the more effective ending.

---

[3]<u>Ibid</u>., p. 486.

RESOURCES

Much of what has been written on grammar and style does indeed exist in the more traditional grammar books. The problem with these books was that they tried to cover every topic, and often topics were taught and learned in the classroom in isolation, with no real relevance to writing. Additional work on grammar and style maybe found in a myriad of books, including the following:

Davey, Richard. The Writing Process. Scarborough; Prentice-Hall, 1984.

Larock, Margaret H., Tressler, Jacob C. and Lewis, Claude E. Mastering Effective English. Copp, Clark, Pitman, 1980

Some teachers will remember this book and its earlier editions from their high school days. It remains a classic reference on the English language.

Parker, John F. The Writer's Workshop. Don Mills; Addison-Wesley, 1982

Warriner, John E., Whitten, Mary E. and Griffith, Francis. English Grammar and Composition. New York; Harcourt, Brace, Jovanovich, 1977.

Winter, Ernest H. Learning to Write. Macmillan Company of Canada Limited, 1961

These books are somewhat old and have perhaps fallen out of fashion with the move away from teaching grammar in secondary schools. However, many older schools have them stored up in a locked room, and so they may be available for teacher use. They are excellent sources of exercises to complement the style and grammar sections of this resource.

APPENDIX A

OVERHEADS

The following pages are suitable for making overheads for some of the topics included in this resource.

Most of these topics concern the organization of the essay as these are the subjects that will concern most students in a class which is being taught the basics.

Teachers should feel free to make overheads of any other pages in this resource that they may use with an entire class.

THE ESSAY AND THE REPORT

Arguments and Reports differ in **PURPOSE** and in **ORGANIZATION**.

	ESSAY	REPORT
PURPOSE	• to be subjective: to argue a specific point of view • to provide evidence to support this point of view	• to be objective: to present findings from research • to provide examples from the research
ORGANIZATION	• statement of thesis: overall argument and supporting arguments • explanation of each argument in turn, followed by presentation of evidence and examples • conclusion	• statement of scope and purpose of the report • summary of findings citing examples and sources • conclusion and recommendations if required

SAMPLE OF ESSAYS AND REPORT TOPICS

	ESSAY	REPORT
Topic 1: The Senate	• The Senate should be abolished. • The Senate performs a useful check on government	• The organization of the Senate, including number of members, how they are appointed, what areas they represent, etc.
Topic 2: Erosion	• A particular planting technique is more helpful than another in preventing soil erosion. • Many economic disasters might have been averted if farmers had taken measures to control erosion.	• The advantages and disadvantages of various methods to control erosion. • Areas of the earth where erosion poses particular problems to the way of life of the inhabitants.
Topic 3: Women in Literature	• Women in literature are depicted as weak individuals defeated by their environment. • Shakespeare's women are extremes, either pretty ornaments or domineering tyrants.	• Examples of women who have written important pieces of literature and summaries of their lives. • Biographies of female characters in the works of a particular writer.

THE PARTS OF AN ESSAY

The argument of an essay is expressed in what writers call the **THESIS**. A thesis is the expression of the overall argument and the developing arguments of an essay. A thesis consists of two parts: **proposition** and **issues**.

PROPOSITION

is true because

ISSUE 1
ISSUE 2
ISSUE 3, etc.

are true.

The thesis is based on **evidence**. **EVIDENCE** consists of examples, quotations, appeals to authority of any kind, statistics, logic--anything which will prove the validity of an issue.

PREWRITING PLAN

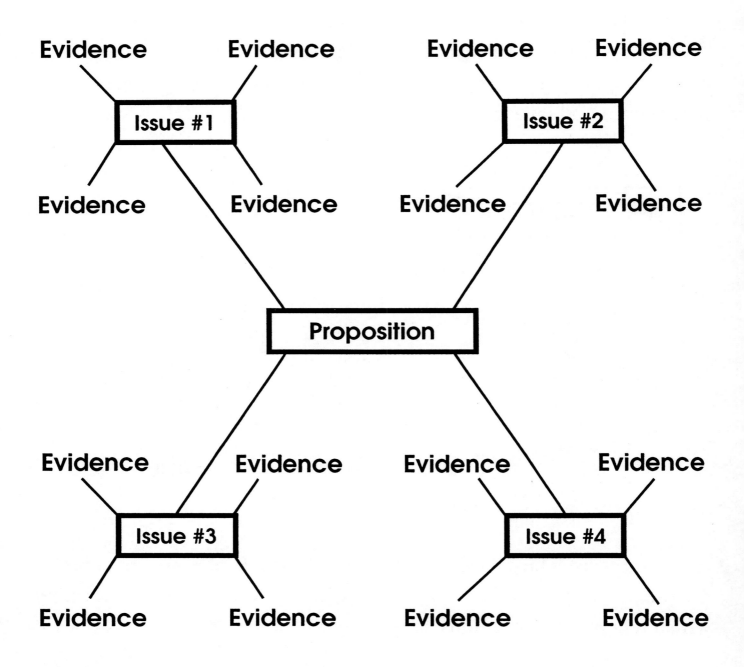

Evidence   Evidence

Issue #1

Evidence   Evidence

Evidence   Evidence

Issue #2

Evidence   Evidence

Proposition

Evidence   Evidence

Issue #3

Evidence   Evidence

Evidence   Evidence

Issue #4

Evidence   Evidence

Publication Listing